T0198833

Hi! I'm Elvis.

Ain't nothin but a hound dog.

Text by
James H. VanSciver, Ed.D.

Photos by
Paula M. VanSciver

To order additional copies of this book, contact:
Xlibris
1-888-795-4274
www.Xlibris.com
Orders@Xlibris.com

ISBN: Softcover   978-1-9845-8878-4
        EBook   978-1-9845-8877-7

Print information available on the last page

Rev. date: 07/24/2020

Thanks to Al Schock for making Elvis possible for us and to Crystal O'Neal for the idea for this book. We would not have otherwise thought of it.

Dedicated to all pets who bring purpose, patience, happiness, and love to their owners.

In memory of our first Sheltie . . . Titan, who will forever hold our hearts.

Hi! I'm Elvis. As I grow up I think of all of the lessons I will learn. Some of them will come from my family and others from my teachers. I've already learned how to sit. There are lots of other lessons I want to share with you. You don't want to end up being nothing but a hound dog.

I like meeting new friends. Most of them look a lot different from me. Some are a different color, others are bigger, and still others have a different kind of hair. It is important to make them all happy.

Chewing is a lot of fun. But, to enjoy it, you have to take care of your teeth. Don't forget to brush each day and floss your teeth.

Another part of being healthy is eating right. I like to mix vegetables and fruit with my meat. That way I get all of the vitamins and minerals my body needs.

Water is important for my health, too. I try to drink as much as I can each day. Water helps clean my body and keep me active.

Another way to keep healthy is to be clean. I take regular baths. Right now, I'm little so I get washed in the sink. Make sure to wash behind your ears!

Sometimes I feel sad. When that happens, I go to my happy place and stay there for a while. It cheers me up.

If I do something I'm not supposed to do, I get sent to my room to think about it. That's why I always try to do what's right.

I really enjoy playing. Anything can be a toy, even an empty plastic soda bottle. The best is pushing it around the room with my nose and then chewing on it. I'm never bored. When all else fails, I can always run in circles trying to bite my tail.

I also like to play tug-of-war. I don't always win but I try to be humble in victory and graceful in defeat. That way I can play again.

When I play, I enjoy myself and my playmate but I don't want to be so rough that I hurt him or myself. Always be safe.

Being nice means sharing and taking turns. That will help your playmate enjoy being with you. That's important to me.

Do you like to go for walks? I do. I really like being out in the fresh air and smelling everything outside. It also is very good for my health to be active.

I also like to keep my mind healthy by reading. You can learn so much from books. Just don't chew on them.

Sometimes I have a lot of fun just rolling on my back and kicking my feet. I don't know why but it just feels good.

Resting is also good for your body. Sometimes I just like to curl up in a nice soft bed and think about all of the fun I am having.

Sometimes I make a mess but I always try to help clean up. It's also important to put your toys away when you are finished playing.

Think about how you dress. You only get one chance to make a good first impression. I only have one outfit so I have to wear it each day. I hope you like it.

Sometimes, I leave my home with one of my ear flaps up and my whole day is off to a bad start. Make sure that you have all of your supplies and completed homework each day before you go to school so that doesn't happen to you.

When the day is over, there is nothing like going to sleep. If you can find a nice soft pair of slippers take advantage of them. Sweet dreams!

There you have it. I'm only eight weeks old but that's how I feel about life. I wish you luck as you grow. Maybe sometime I will get to meet you. If I do, I'll lick your hand. Remember, you don't want to end up being nothing but a hound dog.

Elvis lives with his parents, Paula and James VanSciver, in Lewes Delaware. Paula has raised five children, two dogs and two cats. James has published three other children's books with Xlibris Publishing, *Close Play at Home, Carnage of a Curveball, and Running on Empty*. He has also published an educational leadership book, *Generalities of Distinction*, through Rowman and Littlefield.

You may contact them at
(443) 880-5329 or at paulamv723@gmail.com.

Printed in the United States
By Bookmasters